Lee Canter's Assertive Discipline®

TEACHER'S
MAILBOX

A Collection of Reproducibles to
Facilitate Communication Between Teacher, Student, and Parent

Grades K-6

A Publication of Lee Canter & Associates

CL
CL
371.7
CL

Staff Writers: Marcia Shank, Pat Sarka, Sue Lewis, Rozanne Williams, Carol Provisor
Illustrator: Patty Briles
Editorial Staff: Marlene Canter, Kathy Winberry
Designer: Pam Thomson

© 1988 Lee Canter & Associates
P.O. Box 2113, Santa Monica, CA 90407-2113
(800) 262-4347 (310) 395-3221

Printed in the United States of America
First printing March 1989; Sixth printing January 1992

ISBN 0-939007-11-8
Revised May 1991

TABLE OF CONTENTS

ASSERTIVE DISCIPLINE® AND POSITIVE COMMUNICATION

In order for your students to fulfill their potential, they must have a classroom environment in which they can learn and you can teach. Lee Canter's Assertive Discipline is a behavior management system that enables teachers to have the kind of classroom atmosphere they need to meet goals for themselves and for their students. Rules for behavior are developed, together with consequences for when students break the rules, and rewards for when students observe them. The Classroom Discipline Plan is then communicated to the students, the principal and the students' parents.

Positive communication about behavior is a key component of Assertive Discipline. Both students and their parents need to get the message that positive behavior is being noticed and rewarded in your classroom. How is this accomplished? First of all, verbal praise should become an integrated part of your teaching style. Secondly, positive notes and awards should be given to students on a consistent basis. Thirdly, verbal and written interaction with parents should be ongoing from the beginning of the school year to the end to assure involvement and support. Welcoming notes, positive phone calls, thank you notes, conference reminders— these positive communications will encourage the parent support and involvement you need to achieve the ideal classroom environment.

About Teacher's Mailbox

The reproducible forms in *Teacher's Mailbox* provide you with many ways to communicate in writing with parents—throughout the entire school year. Send parents notes, invitations, newsletters, behavior reports, communication forms and copies of your Classroom Discipline Plan using the reproducibles in *Teacher's Mailbox*. The more you can make parents aware of what's happening with their child, the more cooperation you'll have when you need it.

Teacher's Mailbox has a variety of student notes, awards, cards and communication forms that will help you to keep an open and constructive interaction with your students. To ensure that you are giving positives on a consistent basis, use the documentation sheet to record all positive communications. When you make frequent use of the reproducibles in *Teacher's Mailbox*, the improved learning experience in your classroom will reflect your communication efforts.

PART ONE
Beginning of the Year:

Building Teacher-Parent-Student Communications

"Welcome Back" Letters for Parents and Student

Pages 8 and 9

Take the initiative to make positive contact with your new students and their parents before school begins. To make a positive impression on parents, mail this letter to them before school begins, or send it home with the student on the first day of school. Establishing lines of communication early will pave the way for an ongoing, cooperative relationship between you and your students' parents.

Use the handy fold-a-note on page 9 to write a brief note to each student in your class—just to say "hi" and introduce yourself. Staple shut, address, stamp and mail.

"First Week of School" Notes to Students

Page 10

You can't start too soon giving positive messages to your students. Positive reinforcement is the key to the success of your school year—academically and behaviorally. "Catch" your students being good that first week of school and reward them not only with your praise, but with a positive message home. Share your pride with your students and their families.

Classroom Discipline Plan Letter for Parents

Page 11

During the first week of school, after you have explained your Classroom Discipline Plan to your students, notify the parents about your expectations for their child. When parents know there is a firm plan for behavior management in place at all times in your classroom, you will earn their respect and support. Right from the start, they will have a good feeling about you and the way you conduct your classroom.

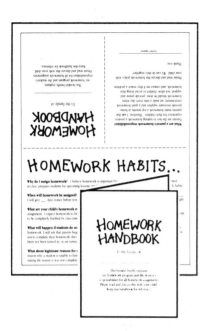

Homewerk Handbook

Page 12

Communicate your homework expectations to students and parents by sending home this helpful booklet. It gives parents the answers to the "who, what, when, why and how" of homework—all in one handy little booklet. The home/school connection is very important to the success of any homework program—so involve parents from the very beginning.

Classroom Volunteer Request

Page 13

When parents take part in your classroom activities, their child is excited and proud of their involvement. Invite parents to help you with Back-to-School Night, Open House, classroom parties, special events, tutoring— anything that will relieve some of your workload. Don't forget to send the special note of appreciation for their assistance on page 52.

Parent-Teacher Communication Cover Letter and Form

Pages 14 and 15

Parental involvement and support are key ingredients for a successful behavior management program. At the beginning of the year, you can establish a positive relationship with the parents of your students by sending home several copies of the Parent-Teacher Communication Form together with the cover letter. Run off the form on bright, easily distinguishable colored paper. Use the form to inform a parent when their child is not following the rules or when you need to ask for a parent's help. These forms are a handy way to tell parents about a student's appropriate behavior, too. The form can be generated from you to a parent, or from the parent to you.

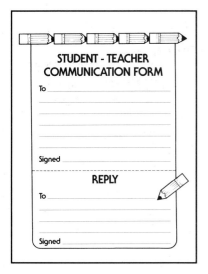

Student-Teacher Communication Form

Page 16

Your students need to know they can express feelings and air problems freely and confidentially. By allowing them to "blow off steam" safely, you can prevent many discipline problems before they begin. Keep a stack of Student-Teacher Communication Forms accessible and encourage your students to use them. The forms can be generated from the student to the teacher, or from the teacher to the student. The top half of the form is for the question or comment, and the bottom half is for the reply. A student with a problem, question or comment can write down the message and place it in a sealed box located in the room. You read the message, then reply.

Classroom Birthday List & Student Birthday Card

Pages 17 and 18

Record each student's birthday on the Classroom Birthday List on the first day of school. Then place the list on a bulletin board or in your plan book. When a birthday arrives, make the most of that happy time by giving your students an extra-special positive message in the form of the Happy Birthday Card. Duplicate the birthday card on construction paper or index card stock. Cut on the solid line and fold in half along the dotted line so that the animals pop up. Write the student's name and sign a personal birthday greeting inside.

Get Well Card and "While You Were Absent" Homework Reminders

Pages 19 and 20

The *Teacher's Mailbox* Get Well Card will demonstrate to students who are "under the weather" that their teacher and classmates are thinking about them. And when your recuperated students return to school, attach this classwork/homework reminder slip to any make-up work.

Positive Communication Tracking Sheet

Page 21

It's important to keep track of your positive reinforcement efforts. Place this handy tracking sheet inside your plan book or tape it to your desk. Each time you send home a note or award, place a positive phone call or reward a student positively, jot down the date in the appropriate box. Reproduce a new tracking sheet each month—and keep up the positive momentum!

Welcome

Greetings from _____!

School Name

To the Parents of _____ ,

I'd like to welcome you and your child to the start of the new school year. We are going to have a busy and productive year, filled with exciting learning activities, social events and so much more.

Throughout the year I will keep you informed of everything that's going on—my classroom plans, your child's progress and all the activities that will make this a successful—and memorable—year.

I am looking forward to sharing this year with you and your child.

Sincerely,

_____

To:

_____

_____

_____

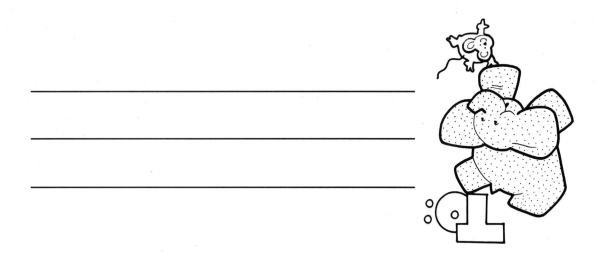

Place Stamp Here

From: _____

_____

_____

To: _____
Student

**You're "on the road"
to a great year!**

_____
Teacher's signature

Dear_____,
Student

"A Star
is born"

**You've made
this first week
of school a real
pleasure!**

Thank you,

_____
Teacher's signature

To the parent(s) of _____,

In order to maintain a classroom that allows all children to learn, I have developed a classroom discipline plan. Please read and discuss the following rules, consequences and rewards with your child.

1. Rules
These rules will be in effect at all times in my classroom:

1. _____
2. _____
3. _____
4. _____
5. _____

2. Consequences
When a student chooses not to follow these rules:

The first time a student breaks a rule _____

The second time a student breaks a rule _____

The third time a student breaks a rule _____

The fourth time a student breaks a rule _____

The fifth time a student breaks a rule_____

* Severe misbehavior such as fighting, threatening students or teachers, verbal abuse or _____
_____ will result in the student being immediately sent to the principal.

3. Students who behave appropriately will be positively rewarded with:

_____

_____

_____

_____

I have discussed this plan with all the students in my class, but I would appreciate it if you would review the rules, consequences and rewards with your child. Then sign and return the form below to school. Keep this portion for your own information.

Thank you for your support. This year will be successful if we work together.

Sincerely, _____
Teacher's signature

- -

I have read the discipline plan and have discussed it with my child, _____

Parent's signature   _____

Date   _____

Comments   _____

Teacher's signature

Thank you,

Please read and discuss this homework policy with your child. We can do this—together!

What are a parent's homework responsibilities? Parents are the key to making homework a positive experience for their children. Therefore, I ask that parents make homework a top priority at home, provide necessary supplies and a quiet homework environment, set aside a time every day when homework should be done, provide praise and support, not allow children to avoid doing their homework, and contact me if they notice a problem.

This booklet briefly explains my homework program and the student's responsibilities for all homework assignments. Please read and discuss this with your child. Keep this handbook for reference.

To the family of

HOMEWORK HANDBOOK

HOMEWORK HABITS...

Why do I assign homework?   I believe homework is important because it helps reinforce what has been learned in class, prepares students for upcoming lessons, teaches responsibility and helps students develop positive study habits.

When will homework be assigned? I will assign homework: _____
I will give ___ days notice before tests. Assignments should take no more than _____ each night.

What are your child's homework responsibilities? I expect students to do their best job on each homework assignment. I expect homework to be neat, not sloppy. All written work should be done in pencil. I expect homework to be completely finished by class time the following morning.

What will happen if students do not complete their homework assignments? If students choose not to do their homework, I will ask that parents begin checking and signing completed homework each night. If students still choose not to complete their homework, they also choose to lose certain privileges. After three homework assignments have been not been turned in, or are turned in incomplete, the parent will be contacted.

What about legitimate reasons for a student not completing a homework assignment? If there is a legitimate reason why a student is unable to finish the assignment, please send a note to me on the date the homework is due stating the reason is was not completed. The note must be signed by the parent.

Dear Parent,

Our class could use an extra pair of hands. We hope you can volunteer. Here's what we need:

_____

_____

_____

_____

_____   Room _____

Student's signature

_____
Teacher's signature

- -

☐ I'd be happy to help. You can count on me to:

_____

_____

☐ Thank you for asking, but I will not be able to help out this time. Please ask me again.

_____
Parent's signature

Dear Parent,

It is my belief that positive interaction between teacher and parent strengthens the feeling of support all children need for success in school. My goal this year is to create an atmosphere of open communication regarding your child's progress and behavior in both home and school.

Enclosed you will find copies of our Parent Teacher Communication Form. Please feel free to use the top half of the form any time you wish to express a comment, a concern or to ask a question about your child, the classroom, or the school. I will use the bottom section of the form to send you a prompt response.

In the same way, any time I wish to communicate with you, I will fill out the top half of the form with my comment or question and will request that you send a reply to me.

I am confident this procedure will lead to improved communication between us. By working together we will be able to better meet the needs of your child.

I look forward to hearing from you.

Sincerely,

_____   _____
Teacher's signature   Room number

PARENT-TEACHER COMMUNICATION FORM

To _____

_____

_____

_____

_____

_____

Signed _____ Date _____

- -

REPLY

To _____

_____

_____

_____

Signed _____ Date _____

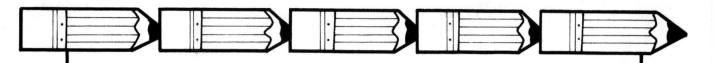

STUDENT - TEACHER COMMUNICATION FORM

To _____

_____

_____

_____

_____

_____

Signed _____

- -

REPLY

To _____

_____

_____

_____

Signed _____

Classroom Birthday List

Date   **Name**

_____   _____
_____   _____
_____   _____
_____   _____
_____   _____
_____   _____
_____   _____
_____   _____
_____   _____
_____   _____
_____   _____
_____   _____
_____   _____
_____   _____
_____   _____
_____   _____
_____   _____
_____   _____
_____   _____
_____   _____
_____   _____
_____   _____

Dear _____
**You are special
in my class because**

_____

Happy Birthday!

Signed _____

Dear _____

Sorry you're not feeling well.

We miss you!

From your classmates in Room _____

and _____

Teacher's signature

School Stuff to do...

To: _____

While you were absent, you missed these assignments:

☐ _____

_____

☐ _____

_____

☐ _____

_____

☐ _____

_____

Complete by _____

Signed _____

School Stuff to do...

To: _____

You need to complete the following homework:

☐ _____

_____

☐ _____

_____

☐ _____

_____

☐ _____

_____

Complete by _____

Signed _____

POSITIVE COMMUNICATION TRACKING SHEET

Student's Name	Positive Note —Student	Positive Note —Student	Positive Note —Parent	Positive Phone Call	Positive Bookmark	MiniGram	Coupon	Other	Other	Other

Month of _____

PART TWO
Back-to-School Night, Parent Conferences, and Other Meetings

Teacher-Parent Communications

Back-to-School Night Invitation

Page 24

Back-to-School Night can be the most important night of the school year. It's your best opportunity to meet parents, explain your policies and programs in detail, and answer any questions about your class. "Roll out the red carpet" by sending these special invitations. Then plan your special night. Prepare an outline of exactly what you will say. Hand out a packet of information that parents can take home with them. Give parents a "tour" of your classroom with a slide presentation and a tape recording of students discussing daily classroom activities.

Back-to-School Night Follow-up Letter

Page 25

Let parents know how much you appreciated their participation in Back-to-School Night by sending home a follow-up note. Use the "Looking Back at Back-to-School Night" note to thank parents for coming and to update them on topics that were brought up at Back-to-School Night. The note includes a section where parents can respond to you with any questions they may have regarding your presentation. This is especially helpful for parents who find it difficult to speak up in a group. This follow-up is also an excellent way to make contact with parents who were unable to attend Back-to-School Night.

School Events Announcements

Pages 26 and 27

For optimum support from parents, keep them informed about school and involved in their child's education. Use these forms to let parents know about special events: Open House, the Spring Concert, Grandparents Day luncheon, the Science Fair, Career Day, etc. You'll get a better turnout if you make your invitation or announcement special. If you involve your students in making the invitations, their enthusiasm may well ignite their parents' interest.

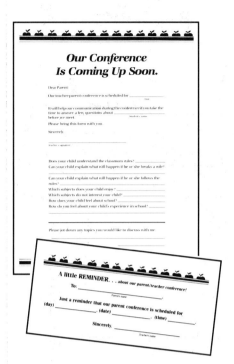

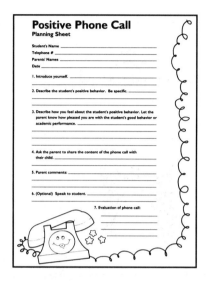

Parent Conference Preparation Form and Reminder Slips

Pages 28 and 29

Use parent conference time wisely by asking the parent to be prepared for your meeting. By filling out this form prior to the conference, parents will be able to clarify some of their thoughts about their child in advance and will feel more confident about meeting with you. After scanning the form, the information may suggest to you a possible new direction for your discussion.

As you receive confirmation from each parent about their parent conference, fill out a conference reminder slip and place it in your plan book. Send home a reminder slip to each parent the day before their scheduled conference. This gentle reminder will stress to parents how commited you are to their child's education.

"Parent Tips for Helping Your Child at Home" Letterhead

Page 30

Many parents want to help their child do better in school, but they just don't know what to do. You can help by giving parents a list of specific ways they can help their children learn at home. Write a list of suggestions on the open-ended "How to Help Your Child at Home" sheet. Some suggestions might include: reading aloud to your child, going to the library together, working with flash cards, encouraging children to write stories, etc. As the year progresses, update the list with specific techniques for mastering current classwork.

Positive Phone Call Planning Sheet

Page 31

A quick phone call updating parents on their child's success in school (academic, behavior or social) is a good habit to establish at the beginning of school—and continue throughout the year. If you make two phone calls a day (each only five minutes in length), you can reach ten parents a week. Once you have established the habit of phoning parents with good news, it won't be so difficult to call them when there is a problem to be solved.

You're invited to Back-to-School Night.

Place _____

Date _____

Time _____

Looking forward to seeing you,

_____
Teacher's signature

Looking Back at
Back-to-School Night

Dear Parents:

Let's keep in touch!
Use this form to write back with any questions or comments you may have.

To: _____

_____

_____

_____

_____

From: _____

Please come to our Open House.

Place _____

Date _____

Time _____

Looking forward to seeing you,

_____
Teacher's signature

AN INVITATION FROM ROOM _____

We have something special
planned in our classroom.
Please join us.

EVENT _____

DATE _____

TIME _____

_____
Student's signature

_____
Teacher's signature

Our Conference Is Coming Up Soon.

Dear Parent:

Our teacher-parent conference is scheduled for _____.
Date

It will help our communication during the conference if you take the time to answer a few questions about _____ before we meet.
Student's name

Please bring this form with you.

Sincerely,

_____
Teacher's signature

Does your child understand the classroom rules? _____

Can your child explain what will happen if he or she breaks a rule?
_____

Can your child explain what will happen if he or she follows the rules? _____

Which subjects does your child enjoy? _____

Which subjects do not interest your child? _____

How does your child feel about school? _____

How do you feel about your child's experience in school? _____
_____

Please jot down any topics you would like to discuss with me.

_____

_____

A little REMINDER. . . *about our parent/teacher conference!*

To: _____,
Parent's name

Just a reminder that our parent conference is scheduled for

(day) _____, (date) _____, (time) _____.

Sincerely, _____
Teacher's name

A little REMINDER. . . *about our parent/teacher conference!*

To: _____,
Parent's name

Just a reminder that our parent conference is scheduled for

(day) _____, (date) _____, (time) _____.

Sincerely, _____
Teacher's name

A little REMINDER. . . *about our parent/teacher conference!*

To: _____,
Parent's name

Just a reminder that our parent conference is scheduled for

(day) _____, (date) _____, (time) _____.

Sincerely, _____
Teacher's name

Parent Tips for Helping Your Child at Home

Positive Phone Call
Planning Sheet

Student's Name _____

Telephone # _____

Parents' Names _____

Date _____

1. Introduce yourself. _____
_____

2. Describe the student's positive behavior. Be specific. _____
_____
_____

3. Describe how you feel about the student's positive behavior. Let the
   parent know how pleased you are with the student's good behavior or
   academic performance. _____
_____
_____
_____

4. Ask the parent to share the content of the phone call with
   their child. _____
_____

5. Parent comments: _____
_____
_____

6. (Optional) Speak to student. _____
_____

7. Evaluation of phone call:
                              _____
                              _____
                              _____
                              _____

PART THREE
Throughout the School Year:

Positive Communications and Incentives

Monthly Mastheads

Pages 34 - 45

Be as creative as your imagination will allow with the 12 *Teacher's Mailbox* Monthly Mastheads. Here are some ideas. Use Monthly Mastheads:

■ to update parents on your behavior management program.

■ to report classroom news.

■ for children to write stories or poems with a seasonal theme, then bind them together for everyone to enjoy.

■ to report results of behaviors that were worked on during the month.

■ to announce upcoming events.

■ to outline special homework assignments for the month.

■ for students to create class newsletters.

■ for students to collect stickers for positive behavior that month.

Positive Notes to Students

Pages 46 - 48

Every student loves to be told that he or she is special. Recognize your students by giving them one of these awards when they are following classroom rules, using good homework habits or showing improvement either academically or behaviorally. They will be likely to repeat the behavior that earned the award, and your classroom climate will benefit.

Mini-Grams

Page 49

For those days when you don't have time to write lengthy notes of praise to all of your well-behaved students, communicate with *Teacher's Mailbox* Mini-Grams. They allow you to be instantly supportive when your students are following the rules. Run off an ample supply, keep them close at hand—and be generous with them. Your students will take pride in collecting these personal behavior messages.

Positive Notes to Parents about Student Behavior

Pages 50-52

Too often the only news parents receive from school about their child's behavior is bad news. You can do a lot to increase their positive attitude toward school by informing them of good news as well. Send home these positive awards to let parents know about their child's good behavior in the classroom.

Parent Thank-You Note and Awards

Pages 53 and 54

Parents appreciate being recognized for the contributions they make to their child's school. They will be more likely to help out again if they know you value their efforts. Your students will enjoy taking the award home and presenting it. Give special recognition to parents who have:

- ◼ helped out in the classroom.
- ◼ helped with a special behavior problem.
- ◼ brought refreshments.
- ◼ donated supplies.

Coupon Awards

Page 55

Award these coupons to students who have followed your classroom rules for a day (for younger students) or a week (for older students). An opportunity to have 15 minutes free time or to be office messenger for the day will encourage appropriate behavior.

SEPTEMBER

OCTOBER

NOVEMBER

DECEMBER

JANUARY

APRIL

MAY

JUNE

JULY

AUGUST

To _____

Your behavior is out of this world!

Teacher's signature _____   Date _____

HOORAY!

Student's name _____

followed the classroom rules.

Teacher's signature _____   Date _____

CO-PILOT

PILOT

To: _____

Your behavior passes the test with **FLYING COLORS!**

From: _____

Date: _____

GREAT

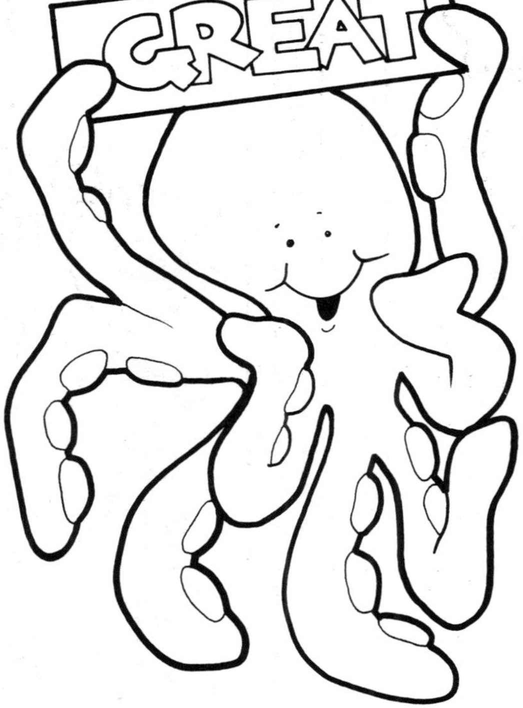

To: _____

I've got to "hand" it to you... You've improved **100%!**

From: _____

Date: _____

COOL

To _____

Your behavior has been real **cool! THANKS!**

From: _____

Date: _____

I'm really PROUD of you, _____,

Student's name

for _____

_____

_____

_____

Thanks,

_____   _____
Teacher   Date

CONGRATULATIONS,

_____!
Student's name

Your hard work has finally paid off! Good Job!

_____
Teacher

_____
Date

MINI-MINI-GRAM

To _____

Thanks for _____

From _____

MINI-MINI-GRAM

SUPER
GRAND
FABULOUS
TERRIFIC
GLORIOUS
WONDERFUL
BEHAVIOR

To _____

MINI-MINI-GRAM

To _____

I spotted you
following the rules!

From _____

Dear _____ ,

_____ **had a**

great day today because

_____

_____

_____

Signed _____

Date _____

Dear _____ ,

_____

followed all the

class rules today.

Signed _____

Date _____

Dear _____,
Thought you'd like to know that
_____ 's behavior
has been outstanding because

_____

_____

_____

Signed _____

Date _____

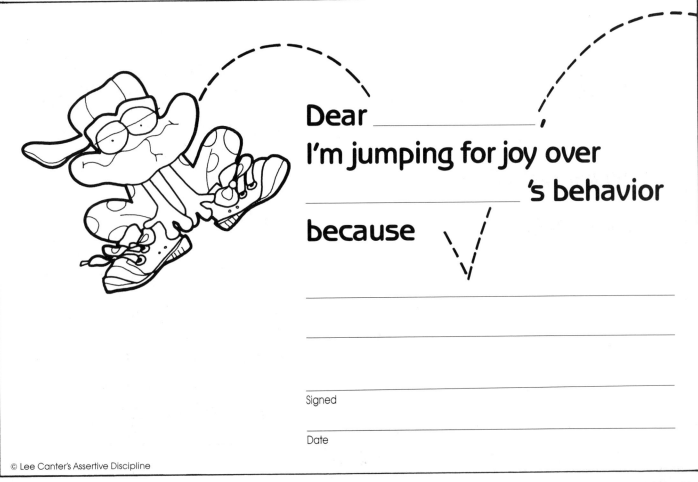

Dear _____,
I'm jumping for joy over
_____ 's behavior

because

_____

_____

Signed _____

Date _____

A Message for You

Wanted You to Know

Dear _____ ,

Thanks for your help in our classroom:

_____

_____

_____

_____

Teacher's signature

Dear Parent,
You're a star because

_____

_____

_____

Teacher's signature

Certificate
of Merit

presented to

_____

_____

for

_____

_____

Student's signature _____

Teacher's signature _____

Date _____

Official Blue Ribbon Award

YOU EARNED IT!

CLASSROOM
MESSENGER

For Your Great Behavior

YOU EARNED IT!

FIRST IN LINE

For Your Great Behavior

YOU EARNED IT!

15 MINUTES
FREE TIME

For Your Great Behavior

YOU EARNED IT!

TEACHER'S
ASSISTANT

For Your Great Behavior

YOU EARNED IT!

15 MINUTES
READING TIME

For Your Great Behavior

YOU EARNED IT!

5-MINUTE CHAT
WITH THE TEACHER

For Your Great Behavior

YOU EARNED IT!

SIT AT
TEACHER'S DESK

For Your Great Behavior

YOU EARNED IT!

For Your Great Behavior

PART FOUR
Throughout the School Year:

Behavior and Homework Reports, Notes and Reminders

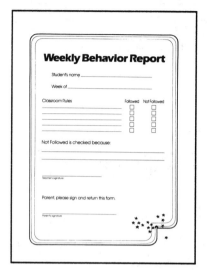

Weekly Behavior Report

Page 58

Parents appreciate specific information about their child's behavior in school. With weekly information, they will be more likely to follow through at home with solutions to problems or with positive support for the child who follows the classroom rules. Run off one copy to use as a master. Fill in the date and the classroom rules. Then run off one copy weekly for each student. Have the parent sign and return the form.

Student Behavior Contract

Page 59

Some problem students need individual attention to help them manage their own behavior. The *Teacher's Mailbox* Behavior Contract is an excellent way to get everybody communicating and working together to help the student. The agreement is signed by the teacher, principal, parent and the student.

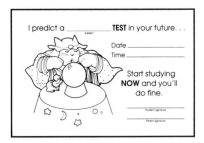

Subject News Notes

Pages 60 - 62

Busy teachers can use all the outside support they can get. You will find that parents who are aware of what's going on in your classroom will be able to communicate with their children about school knowledgeably and confidently, thereby enhancing the child's learning experience. Keep parents informed about what's going on in specific subject areas by using *Teacher's Mailbox* Subject News Notes.

Reminder Notes

Page 63

Use these handy notes to remind students about a variety of things: to bring a particular item to school, to return a message from home, or to bring back a form from home. The "Don't Forget" reminder is great for reminding students and parents of upcoming events, conferences, meetings, school holidays, etc.

Test Update Slips

Page 64

Give your students—and their parents— ample notice of upcoming tests. Send home Test Update Slips several days or weeks before test day. Encourage children to study a little every night instead of cramming—and see the positive results.

Weekly Behavior Report

Student's name _____

Week of _____

Classroom Rules   Followed   Not Followed

Classroom Rules	Followed	Not Followed
_____	☐	☐
_____	☐	☐
_____	☐	☐
_____	☐	☐
_____	☐	☐

Not Followed is checked because:

_____

_____

_____

Teacher's signature

Parent, please sign and return this form.

_____

Parent's signature

BEHAVIOR CONTRACT

Date _____

Student's Name _____

This student has agreed to try to improve his or her behavior and
promises to _____

_____

If the student does as agreed, the student will _____

_____

_____

If the student does not do as agreed, the student will _____

_____

_____

This contract will be in effect for _____

_____   _____
Student's signature   Teacher's signature

_____   _____
Parent's signature   Principal's signature

★ ★ ★

SPELLING NEWS

READING NEWS

LANGUAGE ARTS NEWS

SOCIAL STUDIES NEWS

MATH NEWS

SCIENCE NEWS

Don't Forget...

_____

_____

_____

_____

_____

Signed _____   Date _____

IMPORTANT REMINDER
to bring from home:

_____

_____

_____

Signed _____

_____

Date

It's
TEST TIME
AGAIN!

_____
Subject

_____
Date of test

_____
Student's signature

_____
Parent's signature

© Lee Canter's Assertive Discipline

We've got a DATE on:

_____

for a TEST in:

_____

**Better start
getting ready
NOW!**

_____
Student's signature

_____
Parent's signature

© Lee Canter's Assertive Discipline

I predict a _____ **TEST** in your future...
Subject

Date _____

Time _____

Start studying
NOW and you'll
do fine.

_____
Student signature

_____
Parent signature

© Lee Canter's Assertive Discipline